Science
FOR KIDS

39 Easy
METEOROLOGY
Experiments

Robert W. Wood

TAB BOOKS
Blue Ridge Summit, PA

FIRST EDITION
SECOND PRINTING

© 1991 by **TAB Books**.
TAB Books is a division of McGraw-Hill, Inc.

Library of Congress Cataloging-in-Publication Data

Wood, Robert W., 1933 –
    Science for kids : 39 easy meterology experiments / by Robert W.
Wood.
        p.   cm.
    Includes index.
    Summary: A collection of thirty-nine simple meteorological
experiments, including "How to make a rainbow" and "Why you see your
breath on a cold day."
    ISBN 0-8306-6595-1   ISBN 0-8306-3595-5 (pbk.)
    1. Meteorology—Experiments—Juvenile literature.   [1. Weather-
-Experiments.   2. Experiments.].   I. Title.
QC863.5.W76   1991
551.5'078—dc20
                                       90-21676
                                          CIP
                                          AC

TAB Books offers software for sale. For information and a catalog, please contact
TAB Software Department, Blue Ridge Summit, PA 17294-0850.

Acquisitions Editor: Kimberly Tabor
Technical Editor: Lori Flaherty
Production: Katherine G. Brown   SFK

Contents

Introduction

The Science for Kids series consists of eight books introducing astronomy, chemistry, meteorology, geology, engineering, plant biology, animal biology, and geography.

Science is a subject that becomes instantly exciting with even the simplest of discoveries. On any day, and at any time, we can see these mysteries unfold around us.

The Science for Kids series was written to open the door, and to invite, the curious to enter—to explore, to think, and to wonder. To realize that anyone, absolutely anyone at all, can experiment and learn. To discover that the only thing you really need to study science is an inquiring mind. The rest of the materials are all around you. It is there for anyone to see; you have only to look.

This book, *39 Easy Meteorology Experiments*, is the third in the Science for Kids series and explores one of the most exciting worlds of science—the field of meteorology. Meteorology is the study of the weather and the atmosphere. It attempts to explain why weather conditions occur.

The study of meteorology requires using other sciences, such as physics, chemistry, and mathematics. Meteorologists use physics to explain the movement of the atmosphere; what causes rain, snow, and hail to form; and what lightning and other electrical phenomena are. They use chemistry to study the gases that make up the air we breathe and to study the impurities that pollute it. Mathematics is used to accurately calculate the speed of storms, understand what makes the wind blow, and to make more accurate weather forecasts.

Meteorologists try to learn as much about the atmosphere as they can. They use thermometers to measure the temperature of the atmosphere, barometers to measure atmospheric pressure, and hygrometers to measure its moisture content. Rain gauges are used to determine the amount of rainfall; anemometers and wind vanes are used to measure the speed and direction of the wind.

Airplane pilots, ship captains, farmers, and highway maintenance departments are just a few of the people that are concerned with weather conditions and the science of meteorology. Weather forecasts made by meteorologists even help us decide the clothes we wear, whether to have a picnic or plan a day at the beach, or whether to go on a fishing trip. The first ski trips of the season are planned on a close study of the forecast for snow. Large gas and electric companies use weather forecasts to determine their needs in advance. Even something as advanced as the space shuttle has had its launching delayed by weather. It is easy to see that how we live, where we live, and what we do is, in some way, dependent on weather conditions and the science of meteorology.

The experiments in this book are an easy introduction into the fascinating world of meteorology, but before you begin, be sure to read the *Symbols Used in This Book* section that follows. It warns you of all the safety precautions you should consider before you begin a project and whether or not you should have a teacher, parent, or other adult help you.

Completely read through a project before you begin to be sure you understand the experiment and that you have all of the materials you'll need. Each experiment has a materials list and easy, step-by-step instructions with illustrations to help you.

Although you will want to pick a project that interests you, you might want to do the experiments in order. It isn't necessary, but some of the principles learned in the first few experiments will provide you with some basic understanding of meteorology and help you do later experiments.

Finally, remember that science should be fun. No experiment is ever a failure if you have learned something—even if you learn that something won't work as you predicted. In fact, why not try applying some of your new knowledge about meteorology to deciphering your own local weather and how it affects those in your community. Part II explains how science fairs work and gives you some ideas on how to do a project such as the one I just mentioned.

Symbols Used in This Book

All of the experiments in this book can be done safely, but it is recommended that a parent or teacher supervise young children and instruct them on any potential hazards.

The following symbols are used throughout the book for you to use as a guide to what children might be able to do independently, and what they *should not do* without adult supervision. Keep in mind that some children might not be mature enough to do any of the experiments without adult help, and that these symbols should be used as a guide only and do not replace the good judgment of parents or teachers.

 Electricity is used in this experiment. Young children should be supervised and older children cautioned about the hazards of electricity.

 Materials or tools used in this experiment could be dangerous in young hands. Adult supervision is recommended. Children should be instructed on the care and handling of sharp tools or combustible or toxic materials and how to protect surfaces.

 The use of the stove, boiling water, or other hot materials are used in this project and adult supervision is required. Keep other small children away from boiling water and burners.

 Flame is used in this project and adult supervison is required. Do not wear loose clothing. Tie hair back. When handling candles, wear protective gloves—hot wax can burn. Never leave a flame unattended. Extinguish flame properly. Protect surfaces beneath burning candles.

PART I

METEOROLOGY EXPERIMENTS

1

How Heat Is Transferred by Radiation

Materials
electric lamp
hand

Hold your hand, with the palm up, a few inches under the lamp and turn it on. Notice that you begin to feel the heat almost as soon as you turn on the lamp (Fig. 1-1). The heat is carried to your hand by very short waves of radiant energy. This form of energy can leave its source and travel through empty space at 186,000 miles a second. Radiant energy is not heat, but it can be changed into heat. When it strikes a material that can absorb radiant energy, it makes the molecules that make up the material move faster. This changes the radiant energy into heat energy. The sun warms the earth by radiant energy.

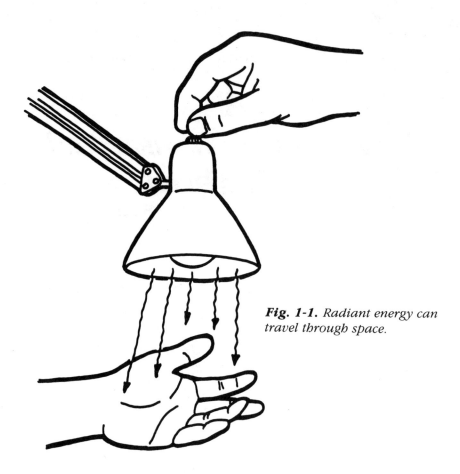

Fig. 1-1. Radiant energy can travel through space.

2

Materials that Absorb Radiant Energy

Fill one can full of water and the other can full of soil (Figs. 2-1 and 2-2). Stand one thermometer in the water and insert the other into the soil (Fig. 2-3). Read the temperatures of the water and the soil. Now place both cans in sunlight and watch the readings on the thermometers (Fig. 2-4).

Notice that the temperature of the soil begins to rise first. This is because the soil absorbs heat faster than water. If the cans are removed from the sunlight and placed in the shade, the soil will also lose heat faster than the water. The wind along a beach blows in different directions from day to night. During the day, the warm earth heats the air above it. This warm air rises as the cooler air from the sea blows in. At night, the wind direction reverses. The earth loses heat and the warmer water heats the air above it. This air rises as the cooler air from the shore blows out to sea.

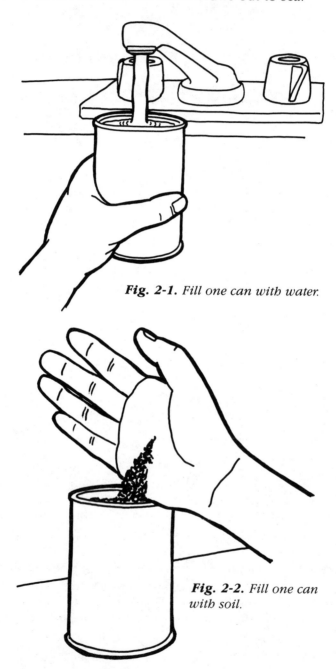

Fig. 2-1. *Fill one can with water.*

Fig. 2-2. *Fill one can with soil.*

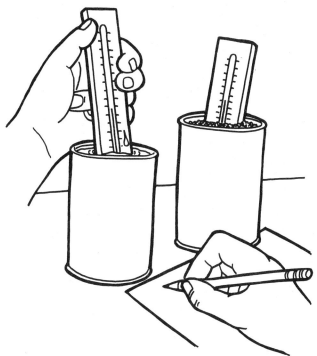

Fig. 2-3. Place a thermometer in each can.

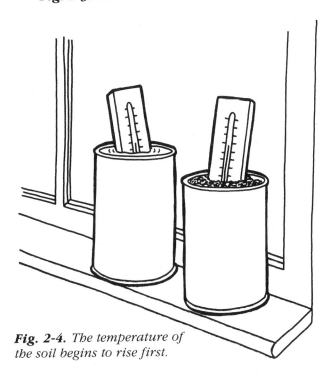

Fig. 2-4. The temperature of
the soil begins to rise first.

3

Temperature Patterns and the Seasons

Materials

Flashlight
Piece of paper

Turn the flashlight on and aim it straight down at the piece of paper. Notice that the light will be concentrated in a circle (Fig. 3-1). Now, hold the flashlight at an angle. The light will be weaker and spread out over a larger area (Fig. 3-2).

The angle that the sun's rays strike the earth is what determines the temperature. Sunshine strikes the earth near the equator from directly overhead, or at about 90 degrees. But near the polar regions, the rays come in more slanted, much less than 90 degrees. This is what causes the difference in the temperatures between the equator and the poles.

The changing angle of the sun's rays also causes the change in the seasons. In the summer, the sun's rays strike the earth at a high angle. The sun's energy is more concentrated and has less atmosphere to travel through. In the winter, the sun is lower in the sky. When the rays are spread over a larger area, they cannot heat the earth as much. The sun's rays must also travel through more of the earth's atmosphere. Much of the energy is absorbed in the atmosphere or scattered back into space, never reaching the earth.

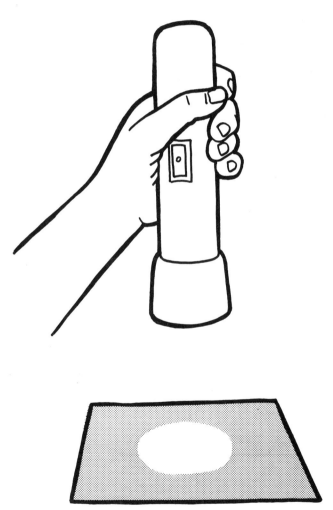

Fig. 3-1. The light is concentrated in a small area.

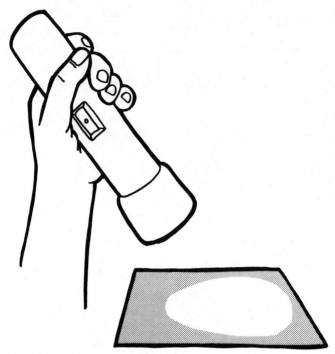

Fig. 3-2. *When the light strikes at an angle, it spreads over a larger area.*

4

The Coriolis Force

Materials

globe
chalk

Place one hand on top of the globe and slowly turn it in the same direction that the earth spins. This will be to the right, or counterclockwise looking down at the North Pole (Fig. 4-1). As the globe turns, drawn a chalk line directly down from the North Pole toward the South Pole (Fig. 4-2). Now, stop the globe and examine the chalk line. It will not be a straight line but a curved one that crosses the equator at an angle. The chalk line will look as if it were drawn from the northeast toward the southwest.

The warm air near the equator is lighter than the cooler air near the poles. Because of this, there is a permanent low-pressure

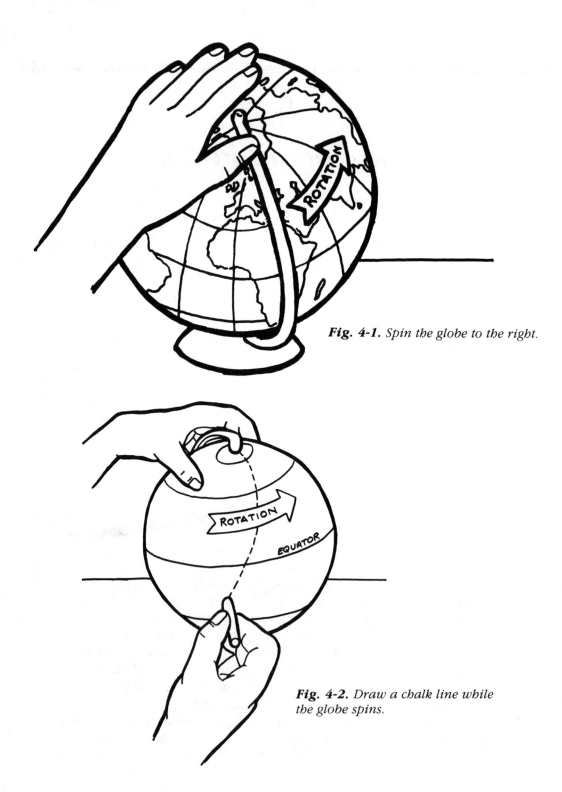

Fig. 4-1. *Spin the globe to the right.*

Fig. 4-2. *Draw a chalk line while the globe spins.*

area around the earth near the equator called the equatorial low. The cooler air at the poles sinks to the earth, forming areas of polar highs. This heavier air moves toward the equator forcing the warmer air upward into the upper atmosphere. This warm air in the upper atmosphere now moves toward the poles. Air moves from the poles to the equator and back to the poles in a continuous cycle (Fig. 4-3).

Air masses do not move directly north or south, however. The rotation of the earth creates a force called the Coriolis force. This force causes the air currents to curve to the right of the direction that they are traveling in the Northern Hemisphere and curve to the left of the direction they're moving in the Southern Hemisphere.

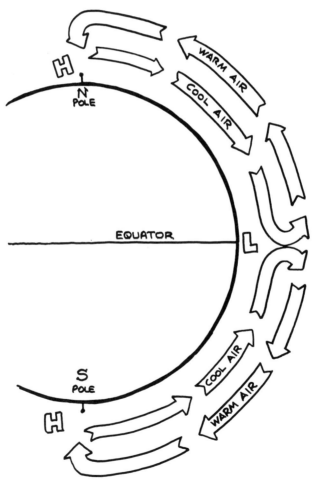

Fig. 4-3. *Air travels back and forth in a continuous cycle.*

This means that the winds blowing toward the equator to replace the rising air are from the northeast in the Northern Hemisphere and from the southeast in the Southern Hemisphere. These winds are called the trade winds (Fig. 4-4).

Over the equatorial regions, air moves constantly upward and is not felt as wind. Sailors call this region the belt of equatorial calms.

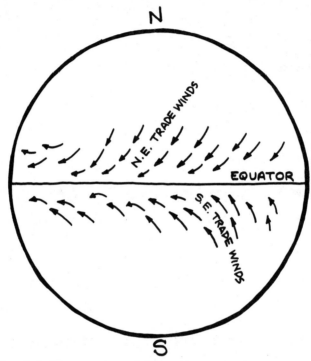

Fig. 4-4. *The rotation of the earth causes the trade winds.*

5

Why Warm Air Rises

Materials

Paper and pencil
scissors
metal thimble
needle
spool (sewing thread)
wood pencil with eraser
table lamp

Mark the pattern of a spiral on the paper (Fig. 5-1). Cut the pattern from the paper but leave enough space in the center to partially insert the thimble (Fig. 5-2). Make the turns about an inch wide. Make a hole in the center and press the bottom of the thimble part way through the hole (Fig. 5-3).

Next, insert the needle upside down into the eraser (Fig. 5-4). Remove the threaded nut from the top of the lamp shade and place the spool over the threaded stud (Fig. 5-5). Place the pointed end of the pencil into the hole in the spool. Carefully set the thimble in the spiral over the point of the needle (Fig. 5-6). The point of the

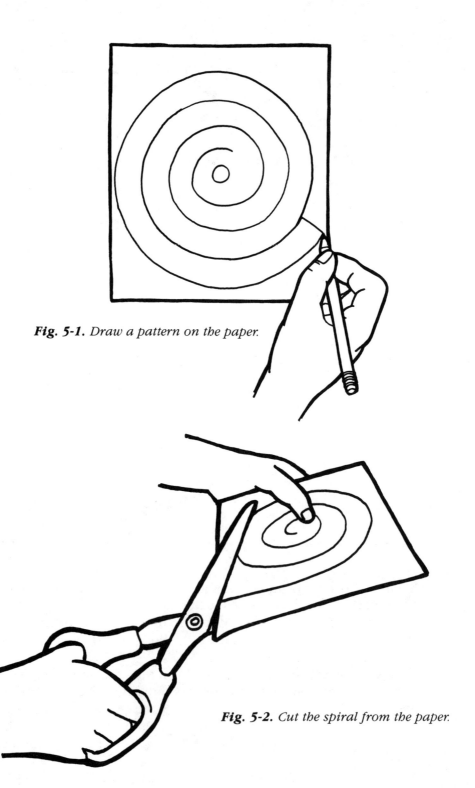

Fig. 5-1. *Draw a pattern on the paper.*

Fig. 5-2. *Cut the spiral from the paper.*

needle makes very little contact with the thimble and this makes a very good pivot point with little friction.

Turn on the lamp and, after a few minutes, the spiral will begin to turn. The lamp heats the air and the molecules of air expand, making the air lighter. Cooler, heavier air moves in and pushes the warm air up. The warm air pushes on the spiral and it begins to turn.

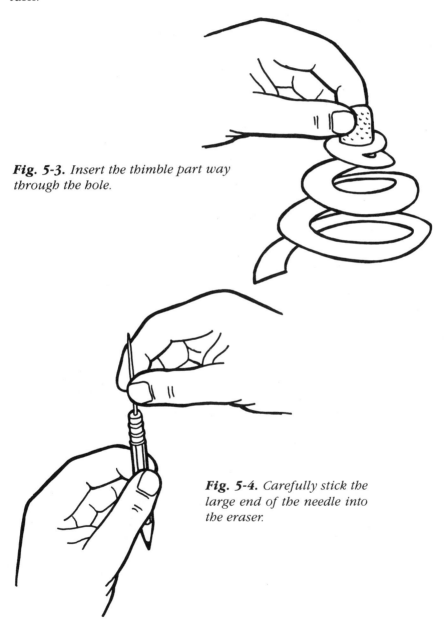

Fig. 5-3. *Insert the thimble part way through the hole.*

Fig. 5-4. *Carefully stick the large end of the needle into the eraser.*

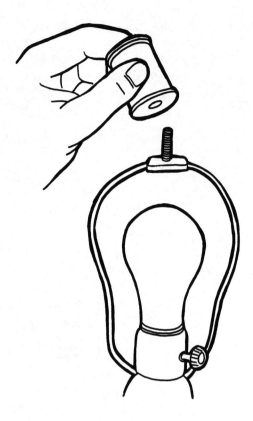

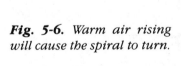

Fig. 5-5. *Place the spool over the threaded stud.*

Fig. 5-6. *Warm air rising will cause the spiral to turn.*

6

Convection Currents

Open the refrigerator door a few inches, and place your hand near the opening at the top (Fig. 6-1). You should feel a warm draft blowing in the opening. Now place your hand at the opening near the bottom (Fig. 6-2). You will feel a cold draft coming out.

When air moves, it becomes wind, or a current of air. When the refrigerator door was opened, the cold, dense air inside quickly moved out into the warmer air in the room. The warmer air was lighter and was pushed up by the cooler air. Warm air from the room rushed into the top of the opening to fill the space left by the cold air. This air is cooled and continues the circulation pattern.

Gravity pulls the cold air down because cold air is dense and heavy. This air moves under the warm air and pushes it up, because warm air is less dense and this makes it lighter. Temperature affects the weather more than anything else.

Fig. 6-1. *Warm air is pulled into the top of the opening.*

Fig. 6-2. *Gravity pulls the cold air down and out into the room.*

7

The Weight of the Atmosphere

Materials

gallon can with lid
cup
water
stove
protective gloves or
pot holders
sink

Pour one cup of water in the can (Fig. 7-1) and, leaving the lid off, place the can on the stove. Have an adult help you heat the water to a boil and, using the gloves, carefully remove the can from the stove (Fig. 7-2). Quickly replace the lid. Now, place the can in the sink and run cold water over the sides of the can (Fig. 7-3). It will instantly collapse because of the air pressure pushing on the outside of the can.

When you suck up lemonade through a straw, you might think that the suction is caused by a pull from the inside of the straw. But what really makes the lemonade go up the straw is a push from the

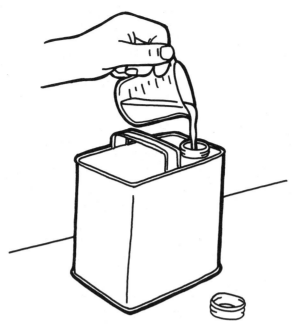

Fig. 7-1. *Pour the cup of water into the pan.*

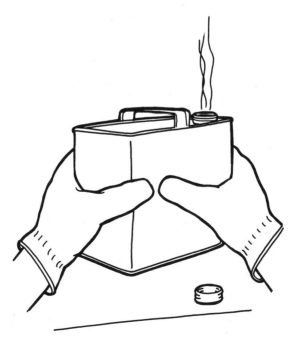

Fig. 7-2. *Use gloves to remove the can.*

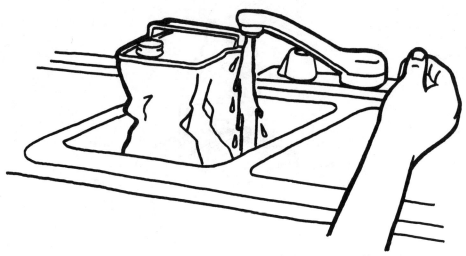

Fig. 7-3. *Atmospheric pressure causes the can to collapse.*

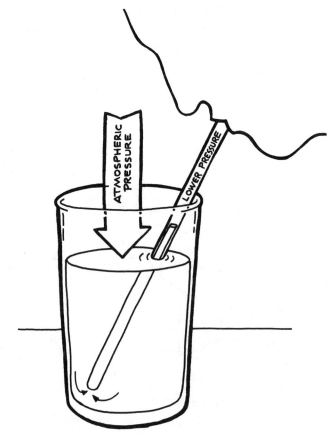

Fig. 7-4. *Atmospheric pressure forces the liquid up the straw.*

outside. Air is pulled down by gravity just like solids and liquids. This downward pull causes air to have pressure. Sucking on the straw lowered the pressure inside the straw and allowed atmospheric pressure to push the lemonade up into the straw (Fig. 7-4).

Our atmosphere surrounds the earth and is divided into four zones: the troposphere, the stratosphere, the ionosphere, and the exosphere. The troposphere is the air from the earth to about 10 miles up; the stratosphere is the air from 10 miles to 60 miles up; the ionosphere is from 60 to 120 miles up; and the exosphere includes all of the air beyond 120 miles above the earth (Fig. 7-5). Atmospheric pressure is measured in atmospheres. An atmosphere is a pressure of 14.7 pounds to the square inch of surface.

Simple lift pumps such as those found in a well use the atmospheric pressure to pump water. It works by removing the air inside the pipe so that the atmospheric pressure pushes water into it. The water comes up the pipe and flows out of a spout. The atmospheric pressure is only great enough to push water up about 34 feet. When the cylinder of a lift pump is more than about 34 feet above the water in a well, it can't pump any water.

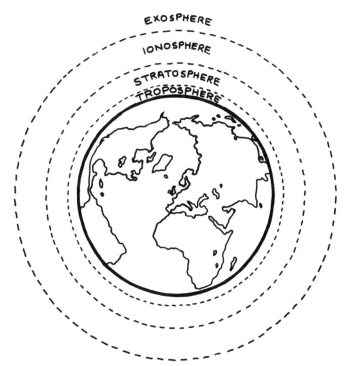

Fig. 7-5. *Our atmosphere is divided into zones.*

8

Compressed Air Is Heavier

Materials

1 yardstick
2 balloons
3 strings (each about 18 inches long)

paper clip
pin or needle
chair or rod

Tie one end of the strings around the exact center of the yardstick (Fig. 8-1). Tie the other end to the back of a chair or a rod so that the yardstick is suspended freely and can be balanced (Fig. 8-2).

Blow up both balloons to about the same size and tie off the openings. Use the two remaining strings to suspend a balloon from each end of the yardstick. One balloon will probably be heavier than the other, so attach the paper clip to the yardstick and move it along until the yardstick balances (Fig. 8-3).

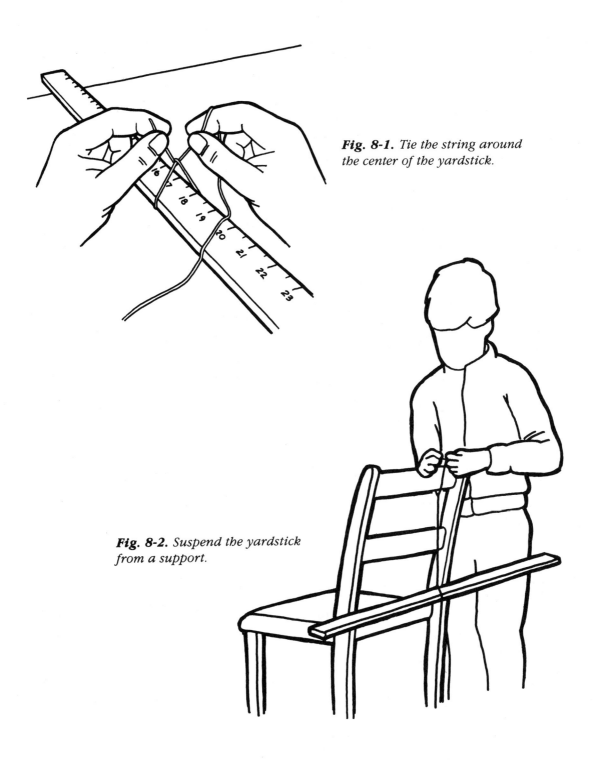

Fig. 8-1. Tie the string around the center of the yardstick.

Fig. 8-2. Suspend the yardstick from a support.

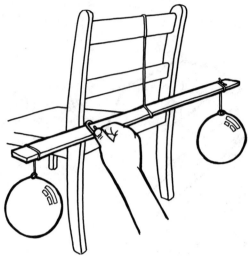

Fig. 8-3. Move the paper clip to balance the balloons.

Use the pin or needle to puncture one of the balloons. The yardstick is no longer balanced (Fig. 8-4). This means that compressed air (the air trapped in the balloon) has weight and weighs more than an equal volume of normal air.

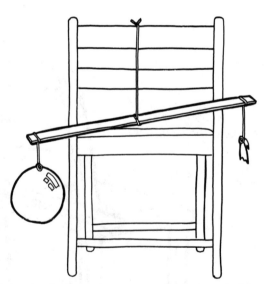

Fig. 8-4. When one balloon was popped, the yardstick was no longer balanced.

═══ **Experiment** ═══

9

How to Pour Cold Air

Materials

large jar with lid
small piece of paper
match
refrigerator
(freezer section)

Wad up the small piece of paper and carefully light it with the match. Blow out the paper (Fig. 9-1) and drop it in the jar. You want to capture the smoke, so quickly replace the lid (Fig. 9-2). Place the jar in the freezing compartment of the refrigerator (Fig. 9-3). After about 10 minutes, take the jar into a room where there are no drafts. Remove the lid. Very little of the smokey air will come out. Turn the jar upside down. The smoke will pour out and sink toward the floor (Fig. 9-4).

The cold air in the jar is more dense than the warmer air in the room. The more dense it is, the heavier it is. Therefore, when you opened the jar right side up, little of the smokey air was able to rise out of the jar. But when you turned the jar upside down, the denser, heavier air sank.

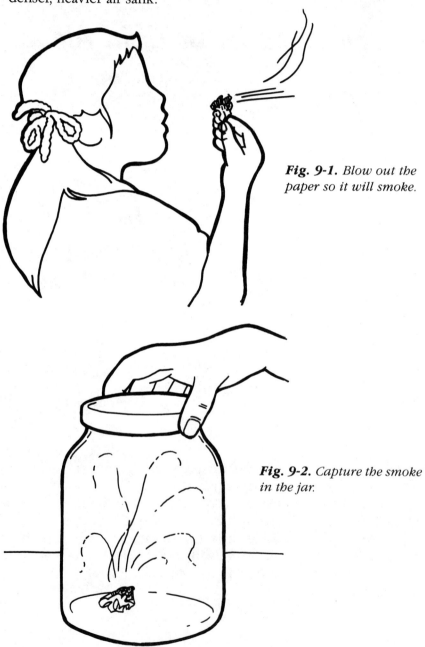

Fig. 9-1. *Blow out the paper so it will smoke.*

Fig. 9-2. *Capture the smoke in the jar.*

Fig. 9-3. *Cool the air inside the jar.*

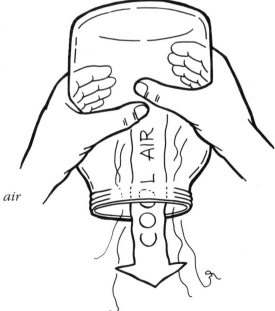

Fig. 9-4. *Pour the cold air from the jar.*

10

How Temperature Affects Air Molecules

Materials

balloon
tape measure
refrigerator

Blow up the balloon and tie a knot in the opening (Fig. 10-1). You don't want it to leak. Place the tape measure around the balloon and measure its circumference (Fig. 10-2). Place the balloon in the refrigerator for about a half hour (Fig. 10-3). Remove the balloon and measure it again. It will be much smaller (Fig. 10-4).

When you blew up the balloon, you used the warm air from your mouth and lungs. When this air cooled, the molecules, or tiny particles, making up the air became smaller and more dense. This means that they took up less space and made the balloon smaller.

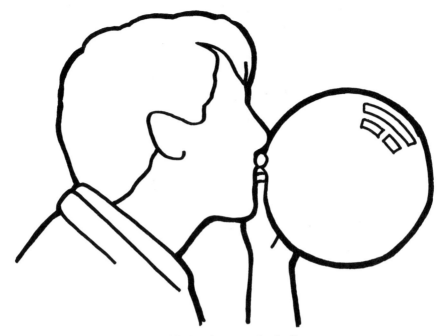

Fig. 10-1. *Blow up the balloon.*

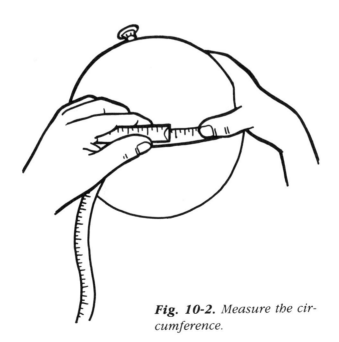

Fig. 10-2. *Measure the cir-*
cumference.

Fig. 10-3. *Cool the air in the balloon.*

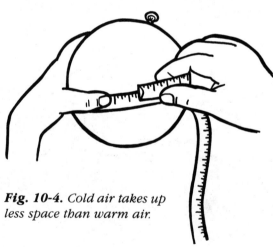

Fig. 10-4. *Cold air takes up less space than warm air.*

11

How Evaporation Cools

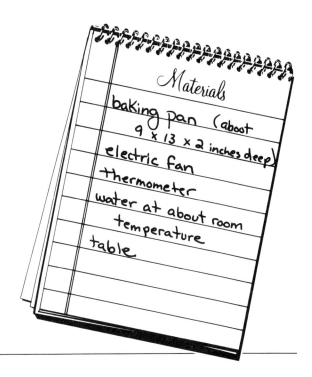

Materials

baking pan (about
9 x 13 x 2 inches deep)
electric fan
thermometer
water at about room
temperature
table

Place the pan on the table and fill it about half full of water (Fig. 11-1). Measure the temperature of the water (Fig. 11-2). Now place the fan on the table so that it blows across the water. **Keep the fan itself away from the water. Electricity and water can be very dangerous. NEVER let electricity come into contact with water**. Turn on the fan (Fig. 11-3) and measure the temperature of the water again (Fig. 11-4). It should become cooler.

The molecules (tiny particles) that make up water are constantly moving. Some of them escape from the surface of the water into the air above. This happens during normal evaporation, but when the air above the water is moving, more molecules escape. The temperature of the water becomes cooler because the heat is absorbed from the water as it evaporates. The more rapid the evaporation, the greater the cooling.

Fig. 11-1. *Fill the pan about half full of water.*

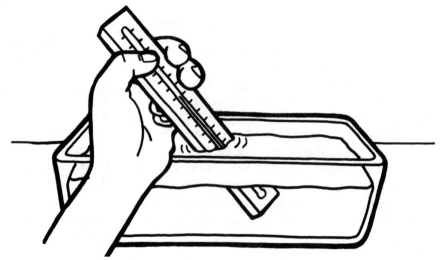

Fig. 11-2. *Measure the temperature of the water.*

Fig. 11-3. *Blow a stream of air over the water.*

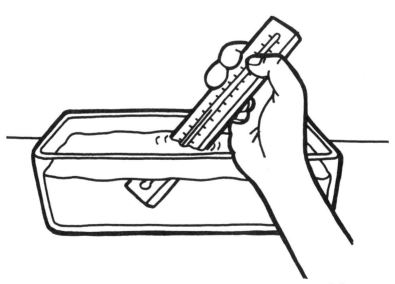

Fig. 11-4. *Air blowing over water lowers the temperature of the water.*

12

Comfort and Humidity

Materials

Plastic bag or empty
bread wrapper

tape
water at about room
temperature

Place one hand in the plastic bag and seal it snugly around your arm with tape (Fig. 12-1). Try to make the bag airtight. Leave the bag in place a few minutes and you will see your hand begin to sweat and become wet. Now, wet your other hand with the warm water. Both hands are wet, but the one in the bag feels uncomfortable while the other hand feels cool (Fig. 12-2).

Humidity is a term that describes the amount of water vapor in the air. If the air contains a lot of moisture, the humidity is said to be high. When it contains only a little moisture, the humidity is low. When the air holds as much moisture as it can, and at a certain temperature and pressure, the air is saturated, or at the dew point.

The amount of moisture in the air compared to the amount required for saturation is called the relative humidity. That is, when the air contains only half of the moisture it can hold, the relative humidity is 50 percent.

Your hand in the bag feels sticky and uncomfortable because the humidity is too high. This keeps the perspiration from evaporating and cooling your skin like the moisture on your other hand.

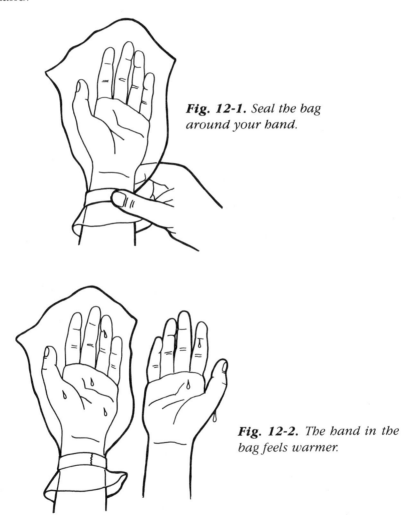

Fig. 12-1. Seal the bag around your hand.

Fig. 12-2. The hand in the bag feels warmer.

13

Why You See Your Breath on a Cold Day

Materials

drinking glass
ice cubes

Fill the glass about half full of ice cubes (Fig. 13-1) and gently blow over the rim of the glass (Fig. 13-2). You will see your breath coming up from inside the glass.

The air you breathe out from your lungs is warm and moist. The ice cubes cooled this air, much like a cold day. Cold air cannot hold as much moisture as warm air, so some of the moisture in your breath condensed into tiny droplets that you can see.

Fig. 13-1. Place a few ice cubes in a glass.

Fig. 13-2. Gently blow over the top of the glass.

14

Why Lakes Don't Freeze Solid

Materials

clear glass bowl
water
refrigerator
(freezing compartment)

Place a bowl about half full of water in the freezing compartment of the refrigerator (Fig. 14-1). Let it stand until ice forms on the surface. Remove the bowl and examine the ice (Fig. 14-2). You will see that the water expanded, or spread out, when it froze. The expanded ice on top of the water is less dense than the water below because it is spread out more. This makes the ice form on the surface.

Water is one of the few things that expands when it freezes. Most things contract, or get smaller, when their temperature is lowered and expand when they are heated. At temperatures above

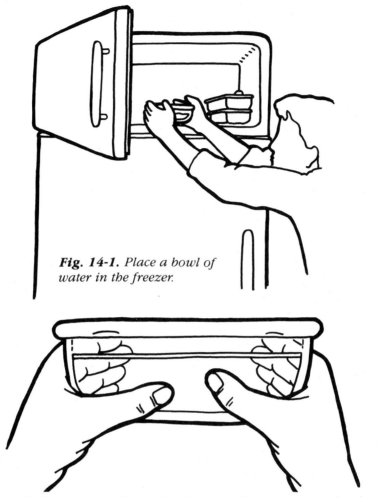

Fig. 14-1. *Place a bowl of water in the freezer.*

Fig. 14-2. *Ice forms on the surface because the water expands when it freezes.*

32 degrees, the molecules that make up water are always in motion. When the temperature drops, the molecules begin to slow down until the water reaches 32 degrees. At this point, the molecules almost stop moving and crystallize into ice.

The ice floats on the water and the surface of the water freezes. As the ice thickens, it insulates the water below it and keeps the water at a temperature above freezing. If it did not float, ice that formed in cold weather would sink and rivers, lakes, and even a large part of the ocean would freeze solid in winter. Fish could not live and there would be very little other water life.

15

How to Make a Rainbow

Materials

garden hose with
spray nozzle

sunlight

Adjust the spray on the hose to a fine mist. Turn your back to the sun and spray the water up in the air in front of you. You should see an arch of brilliant colors (Fig. 15-1).

Rainbows are formed by the sun's rays when they are bent as they strike the drops of water. Rainbows give off seven colors: violet, indigo, blue, green, yellow, orange, and red. You can only see the colors that bend in your direction.

The height of a rainbow depends on how high the sun is. The higher the sun, the lower the rainbow. If the sun is higher than 40 degrees, you will be unable to see a rainbow.

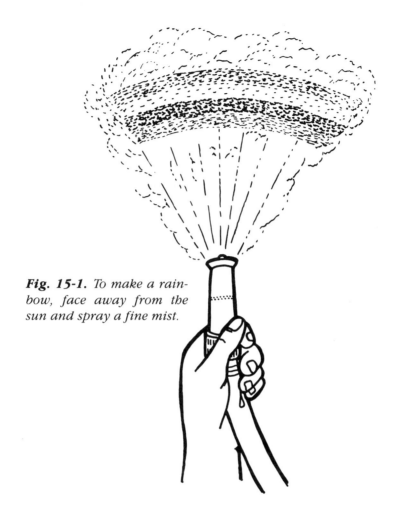

Fig. 15-1. *To make a rainbow, face away from the sun and spray a fine mist.*

16

Cloud Formations

Materials

notebook
pencil
several cloudy days

Watch the clouds and see if you can break them down into these four groups:

1. Stratus clouds normally form only a few 100 feet above the ground. They are thin, billowy, foglike clouds that you sometimes see filling valleys. They are usually seen in early morning or late evening when the air is still (Fig. 16-1). The air often becomes calm at this time of day. The angle of the sun is low enough that the sun's energy is not heating the earth and creating winds.

STRATUS

Fig. 16-1. *Top view of stratus clouds.*

2. Cumulus clouds are fluffy white clouds that drift across the sky about a mile above the earth (Fig. 16-2). On a summer day, they make fast moving shadows across the ground. They increase in numbers and become larger as the sun reaches its warmest in the afternoon. By evening, they usually thin and flatten into stratus clouds. A large number of heavy, cumulus clouds often means rain is in the forecast.

3. Nimbus clouds are dark gray clouds. They are the rain clouds. They tend to have shapeless formations and often blanket the sky. The bottom half of the cloud is filled with moisture that usually turns into raindrops (Fig. 16-3).

4. Cirrus clouds are feathery, white clouds that are made up of ice crystals (Fig. 16-4). They are the highest clouds in the sky, sometimes rising as high as 10 miles above the earth.

CUMULUS

Fig. 16-2. *Cumulus clouds become larger in the afternoon.*

NIMBUS

Fig. 16-3. *Nimbus clouds often mean rain is coming.*

CIRRUS

Fig. 16-4. Cirrus clouds are high, feathery clouds.

Clouds are often classified into four groups according to the heights at which they form.

1. Stratocumulus. Stratocumulus are rain clouds that range from near the ground to about 6,500 feet (Fig. 16-5).

2. Altostratus. Altostratus is a thick, blue-gray cloud blanket that is found from 6,500 feet to 20,000 feet (Fig. 16-6).

3. Altocumulus. Altocumulus clouds are made up of small, white or gray cumulus clouds (Fig. 16-7). These small cumulus clouds are packed close together and form a gray mass that can be found at heights of 8,000 to 20,000 feet.

4. Cumulonimbus. Cumulonimbus clouds are often called thunderheads. They are giant, cauliflower-shaped clouds that can reach heights of up to 11 miles (Fig. 16-8). These towering clouds usually bring thunderstorms with rain, snow, or hail.

STRATO-CUMULUS

Fig. 16-5. *Stratocumulus clouds are water-droplet clouds.*

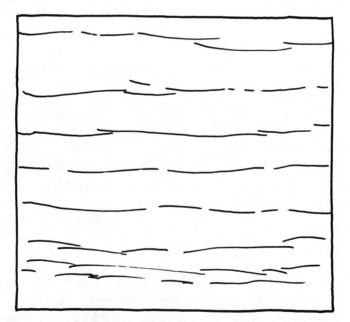

ALTO-STRATUS

Fig. 16-6. *Altostratus clouds form thick, blue-gray blankets.*

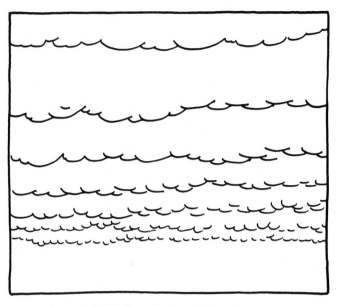

ALTO - CUMULUS

Fig. 16-7. *Altocumulus clouds are round, white, or grayish masses of small cumulus clouds.*

CUMULO - NIMBUS

Fig. 16-8. *Cumulonimbus clouds can be found at all cloud levels.*

17

Dew Point

Materials

tin can or metal cup
thermometer
tablespoon
ice cubes
paper towel
bowl
cool water
salt

The ice cubes should be broken into smaller pieces. Lay the paper towel across one hand and place an ice cube on the towel. Hit the ice cube sharply with the back side of the spoon (Fig. 17-1). The ice cube will shatter into smaller pieces. Place these pieces into the bowl. Continue breaking the ice until you have about half a bowl full of crushed ice.

Make sure that the outside of the can is dry and then fill it about one-fourth full of cool water (Fig. 17-2). Place the thermometer in the can. Add a tablespoon of crushed ice (Fig. 17-3) and stir. Continue to slowly add ice and stir until a thin layer of moisture, or

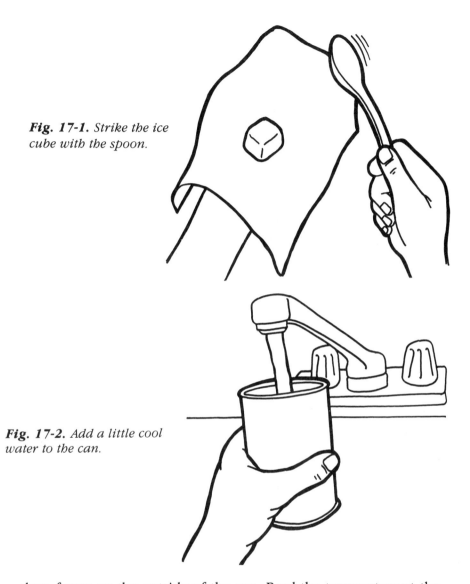

Fig. 17-1. *Strike the ice cube with the spoon.*

Fig. 17-2. *Add a little cool water to the can.*

dew, forms on the outside of the can. Read the temperature at the instant the dew forms (Fig. 17-4). This is the dew point. Add salt to the ice and continue stirring (Fig. 17-5). The moisture will turn into frost because the salt lowered the temperature of the dew to freezing.

Meteorologists find the dew point of air by cooling the air until its water vapor begins to condense. The dew point temperature is not a fixed temperature but changes from day to day. It depends on the amount of moisture in the air.

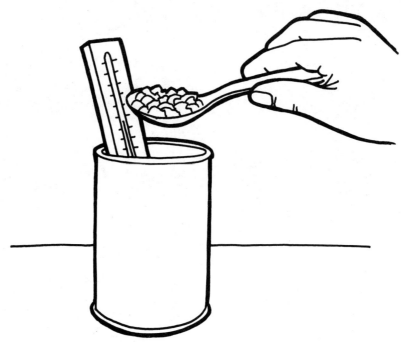

Fig. 17-3. *Add one teaspoon of crushed ice.*

Fig. 17-4. *The dew point is the temperature reading the instant moisture forms.*

Fig. 17-5. *Salt will cause the moisture to freeze.*

18

How to Make a Cloud

Materials

glass jug with a small mouth

match or candle

Turn the jug upside down and carefully hold the opening over the flame of a match or candle (Fig. 18-1). Warm the air inside the jug a few seconds then quickly place your mouth inside the opening to make a seal, then blow hard into the jug (Fig. 18-2). Compress the air inside the jug as much as possible, but be careful not to breathe in. Now, quickly remove your mouth and release the pressure. A cloud will form inside the jug (Fig. 18-3).

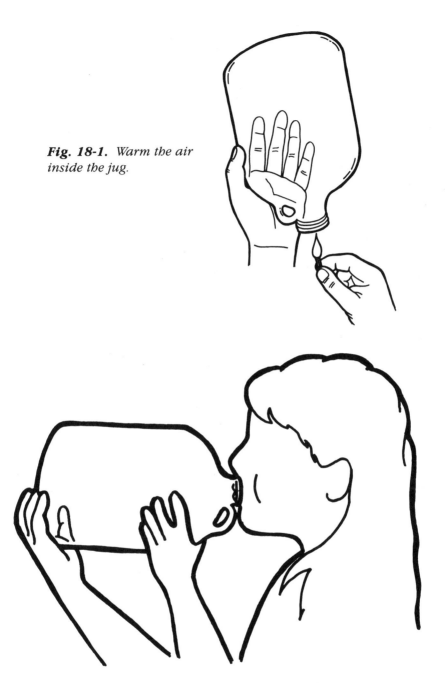

Fig. 18-1. *Warm the air inside the jug.*

Fig. 18-2. *Compress the air inside the jug.*

When you compressed the air in the jug, you also added moisture from your breath. When you suddenly released the pressure, the air in the jug expanded and cooled. The air couldn't hold as much moisture as the warmer air and some of the moisture condensed into tiny droplets and formed a cloud.

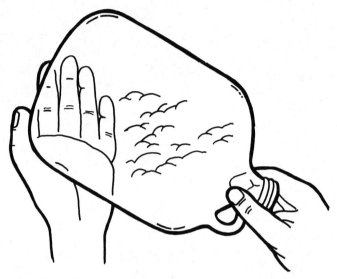

Fig. 18-3. *The air expands and cools, forming a cloud.*

19

How to Make Fog

Materials

clear glass jar
tea strainer
ice cubes
hot water

Fill the jar about half full of hot water (Fig. 19-1). Place the tea strainer over the opening so that the opening is filled (Fig. 19-2). Fill the tea strainer with ice cubes (Fig. 19-3), and fog will form inside the jar (Fig. 19-4).

The warm air from the water was cooled by the air from the ice. The warm air was saturated with moisture and was cooled below its dew point. Water vapor then condensed into tiny drops of water that were suspended in the air and a fog formed. Fog is just a cloud close to the ground.

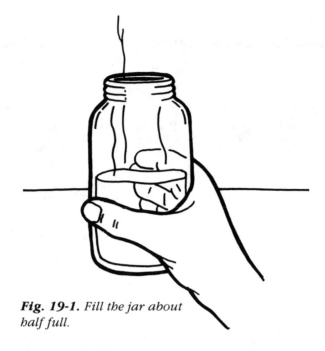

Fig. 19-1. *Fill the jar about half full.*

Fig. 19-2. *Put the tea strainer on top.*

Fig. 19-3. *Add a few ice cubes.*

Fig. 19-4. *Fog will form in the jar.*

20

How Water Gets into the Air

Materials

2 jars the same size (one with a lid)

marking pencil

water

Fill both jars about half full of water (Fig. 20-1). Mark the water level on each jar (Fig. 20-2). Put the lid on one of the jars and leave the other jar open (Fig. 20-3). Let the jars stand side by side for several days. Check the water levels each day and mark any changes in the level. The water level in the open jar will keep falling (Fig. 20-4). Which jar has the air that contains the most water vapor? Is this air saturated?

Water does not evaporate at the same rate every day. It depends on the temperature of the air. The air in the sealed jar became saturated, and when the air is saturated, no more water can evaporate in that air. The warmer the air, the more moisture it can hold. For example, a cubic foot of saturated air at 90 degrees contains five times as much moisture as saturated air at 40 degrees.

Fig. 20-1. Fill the jars about half full of water.

Fig. 20-2. Mark the levels of the water.

Fig. 20-3. *Put the lid on one of the jars.*

Fig. 20-4. *Water does not evaporate when the air becomes saturated.*

21

How to Make Rain

Materials

empty mayonnaise
jar with metal lid
cup of water
fine sandpaper
large nail
hammer
small pot
ice cubes
salt
stove and pot holders

Use the sandpaper to remove the paint from the top of the lid (Fig. 21-1). Try to make the top shiny. Next, carefully use the hammer and nail to make five or six dimples on the inside of the lid (Fig. 21-2). You want the points sticking up on the top of the lid. Be careful not to poke holes through the lid. It shouldn't leak. If you do accidentally make a hole, have an adult help you seal it on the inside with melted candle wax.

Pour a cup of water in the pot and have an adult help you bring it to a boil. Pour the hot water in the jar (Fig. 21-3) and place the lid, upside down, on the opening of the jar (Fig. 21-4). Be sure to use pot holders so you won't burn your hands.

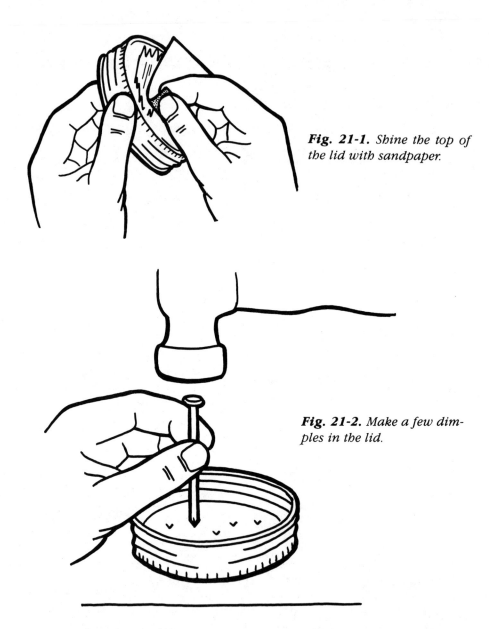

Fig. 21-1. *Shine the top of the lid with sandpaper.*

Fig. 21-2. *Make a few dimples in the lid.*

Place ice cubes in the lid, add a little water and salt (Fig. 21-5), and gently stir (Fig. 21-6). Try to keep the mouth of the jar covered with the lid. Moisture will quickly form on the inside of the jar. Let the jar stand a few minutes and you will begin to see drops falling from the lid. It won't be a steady drizzle, but drops will form on the points on the lid and fall to the water below.

Fig. 21-3. Add hot water.

Fig. 21-4. Place the lid upside down on the jar.

Fig. 21-5. *Add ice cubes and a little salt.*

Fig. 21-6. *Gently stir the ice cubes and moisture will form in the jar.*

When you poured the hot water into the jar, the air in the jar became saturated with moisture. This rose and came in contact with the lid, where it was cooled by the ice. Water condensed on the lid until drops formed on the points and fell.

The warm air rises and carries moisture with it. This moisture-laden air expands and becomes colder as it rises. As the air rises and cools, the amount of moisture it can hold decreases. If this continues, the air becomes saturated. If the air is cooled enough to reach its dew point, clouds form. If the cloud continues to cool, tiny drops of moisture come together and collect on dust particles in the air. Soon they form into drops so large and heavy that they fall as rain.

22

How to Make a Humidity Indicator

Materials

aluminum foil

piece of newspaper

transparent tape

pencil

scissors

wooden spool from sewing thread

Cut a piece of aluminum foil about 4 inches wide and 10 inches long (Fig. 22-1). Cut a strip of newspaper about 1 inch wide and 10 inches long (Fig. 22-2). Tape the edges of the newspaper down the middle of the aluminum foil. Just tape the edges (Fig. 22-3). Now, trim each edge of the foil so that you have a strip about 1½ inches wide and 10 inches long with paper down the middle of the foil.

Tape one end of the strip to the pencil (Fig. 22-4) and wind the strip snugly around the pencil. Wind the strip so that the paper is in the inside (Fig. 22-5). Stand the pencil up in the hole of the spool

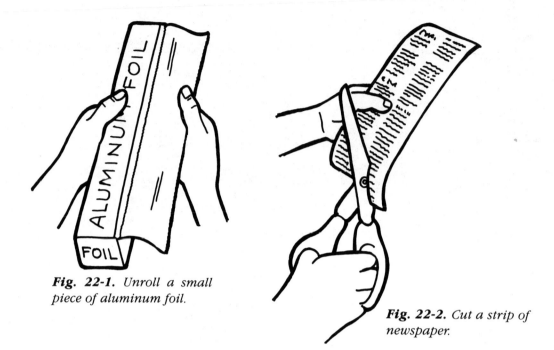

Fig. 22-1. Unroll a small piece of aluminum foil.

Fig. 22-2. Cut a strip of newspaper.

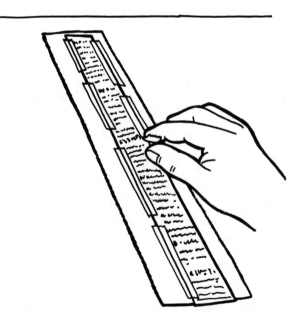

Fig. 22-3. Tape the newspaper to the aluminum foil.

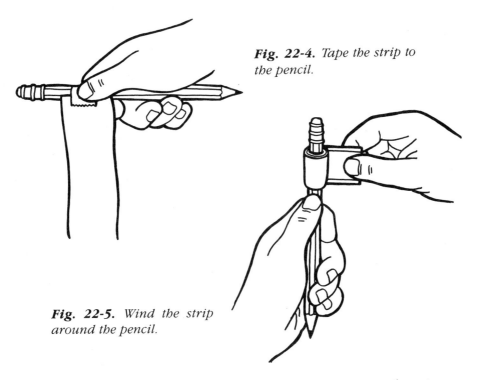

Fig. 22-4. *Tape the strip to the pencil.*

Fig. 22-5. *Wind the strip around the pencil.*

and place it in a moist place like the bathroom (Fig. 22-6). When someone takes a shower, the strip will unwind because of the moisture in the air. When the air is dryer, the strip will wind back up.

The paper absorbs moisture and expands. The aluminum foil cannot. This forces the curl to unwind and wind back up as the moisture content in the air changes.

Fig. 22-6. *The strip will unwind when the moisture in the air increases.*

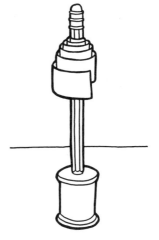

23

Fahrenheit Versus Celsius

Materials

Fahrenheit thermometer
Celsius thermometer
Crushed ice
2 cups

Place a thermometer in each cup and fill the cups with ice (Fig. 23-1). Leave them there for about three minutes then read each thermometer. You will see that the freezing point of water is 32 degrees Fahrenheit and 0 degrees Celsius, or centigrade (Fig. 23-2).

Take your own temperature by placing the thermometers under one of your armpits (Fig. 23-3). The temperature under the arm is normally one degree lower than your actual temperature, so add about 1 °F (0.5 degree C) to the readings taken under the arm. You should have a body temperature of 98.6 °F and 37 °C (Fig. 23-4).

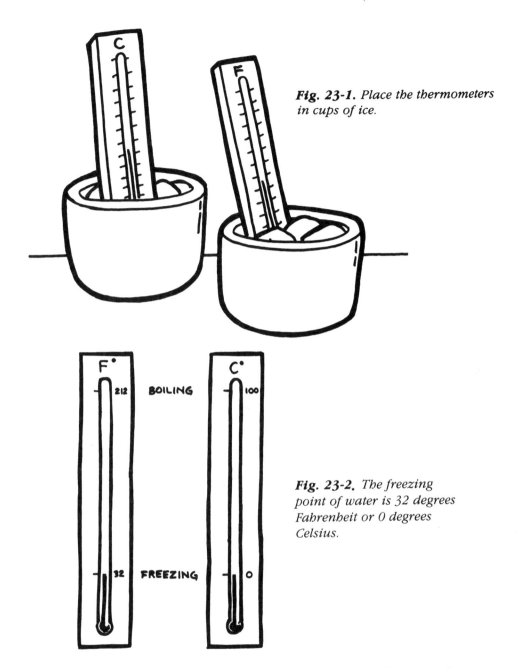

Fig. 23-1. *Place the thermometers in cups of ice.*

Fig. 23-2. *The freezing point of water is 32 degrees Fahrenheit or 0 degrees Celsius.*

Fahrenheit degrees are smaller than Celsius degrees. One Fahrenheit degree equals 5/9 of a Celsius degree. This makes it easy to convert from one to another. To change centigrade to Fahrenheit, simply multiply by 9, divide by 5, and add 32. For example, your body temperature was 37 degrees C. Multiply 37 by 9, which equals 333. Divide 333 by 5, which equals 66.6. Add 32 to 66.6 and you have 98.6, your body temperature in Fahrenheit.

To change from Fahrenheit to Celsius, you just subtract 32, multiply by 5, and divide by 9.

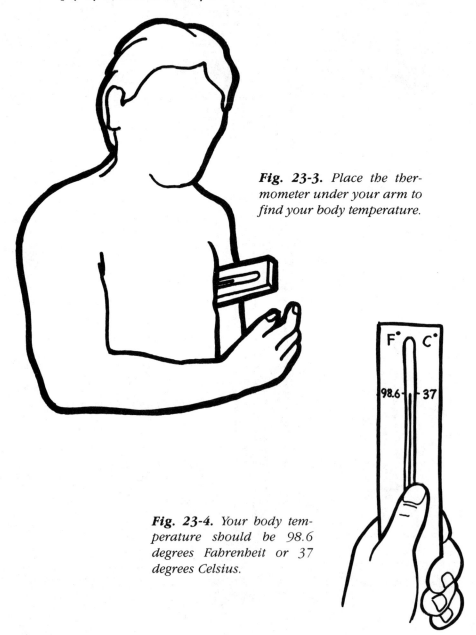

Fig. 23-3. *Place the thermometer under your arm to find your body temperature.*

Fig. 23-4. *Your body temperature should be 98.6 degrees Fahrenheit or 37 degrees Celsius.*

24

Measuring the Temperature of the Air

Materials
thermometer
shade

Place the thermometer in a shady spot about 5 feet above the ground to measure the temperature of the air (Fig. 24-1). In direct sunshine and on the ground, the temperature can be much higher than the actual temperature of the air. As warm air rises, there is less pressure pushing down on it from above. Because there is less pressure, the air expands. As the air expands, it cools. Measurements show that the rising air cools at about 5.5 degrees for each 1,000 feet it rises. When air descends, the air is compressed and becomes warmer. The temperature rises at the same rate of 5.5 degrees for each 1,000 feet it falls.

Fig. 24-1. *Air temperature should be taken in a shady place and above the ground.*

25

How to Make a Thermometer

Materials

Clear glass bottle
(pint or quart)
cork or stopper
with one hole
plastic drinking straw
3x5-inch card and pencil
water
food coloring
candle and matches
transparent tape

medicine dropper
oil

When you choose a bottle, keep in mind that the thinner the glass, the more sensitive the thermometer. Fill the bottle with water and drop in a few drops of food coloring (Fig. 25-1). Push the straw through the hole in the cork (Fig. 25-2), and press the cork into the bottle. If you need to, you can use modeling clay. Just make a clay ball around the straw and make a seal for the opening. The straw should stick down into the water a couple of inches. Carefully light the candle and hold it at an angle so that the wax will drip on the straw and seal the straw to the cork.

Fig. 25-1. *Add a few drops of food coloring.*

Fig. 25-2. *Insert the straw in the hole in the cork.*

The height of the water in the straw should be about one-fourth of the way up the straw. You can use a medicine dropper to add more colored water in the opening of the straw. After adding water to the straw, you can drop in a couple of drops of oil to prevent the water from evaporating (Fig. 25-3). Use tape to fasten the card behind the tube (Fig. 25-4).

To calibrate your thermometer, place another thermometer alongside your thermometer and mark the level on the card. Mark the degrees from the known thermometer (Fig. 25-5). Place the bottle in the shade and in the sun. Mark the temperatures on the card to correspond with those on the thermometer.

Your bottle thermometer works because most liquids expand when heated and contract when cooled.

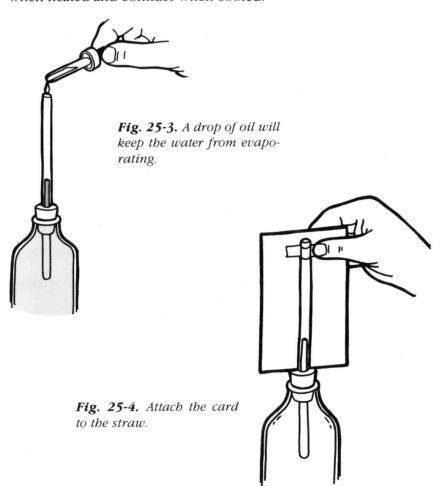

Fig. 25-3. *A drop of oil will keep the water from evaporating.*

Fig. 25-4. *Attach the card to the straw.*

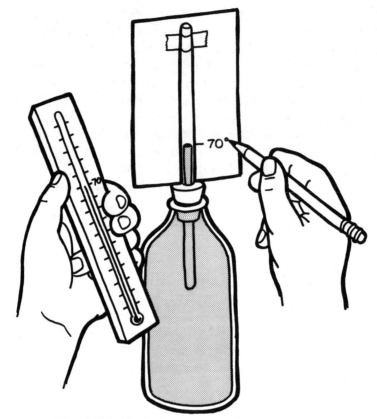

Fig. 25-5. *Mark the temperatures on the card.*

26

Cricket Thermometer

Materials

chirping cricket
watch with second
hand
warm day

Listen for the sound of a chirping cricket (Fig. 26-1). Count the number of chirps in 15 seconds and add the number 37 (Fig. 26-2). This should be about equal to the temperature. Crickets tend to chirp faster as the temperature goes up. In this way, a cricket can act as a live thermometer.

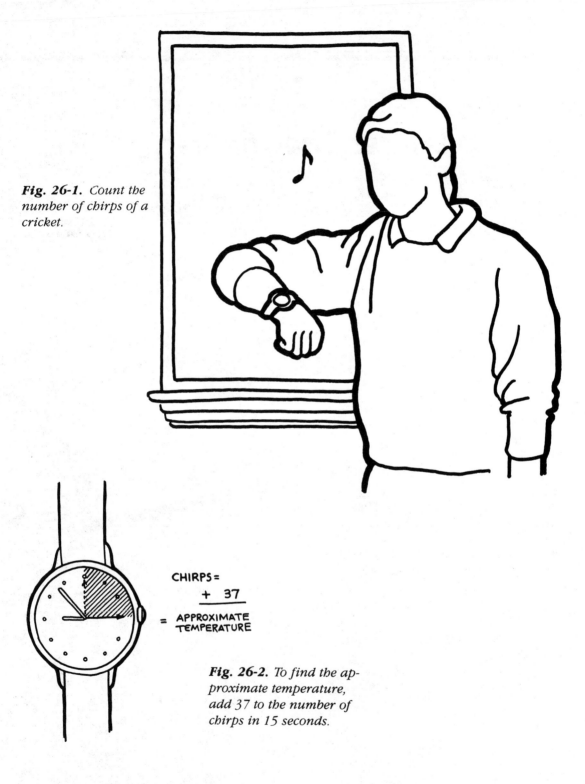

Fig. 26-1. *Count the number of chirps of a cricket.*

CHIRPS =

+ 37

= APPROXIMATE
TEMPERATURE

Fig. 26-2. *To find the approximate temperature, add 37 to the number of chirps in 15 seconds.*

27

How to Make a Wind Gauge

Materials

clear, plastic drinking straw

small styrofoam ball

2 pins

piece of cardboard (about 3 x 12 inches)

transparent tape

exacto knife or scissors

Make the styrofoam ball by cutting a piece from a styrofoam cup, broken ice chest, or food packing material from the grocery store (Fig. 27-1). Use the scissors and cut the ball slightly larger than the straw. Then roll the piece between your finger and thumb until it forms a ball that will roll freely inside the straw (Fig. 27-2). The straw must be clean and dry.

Cut a notch in the straw about a half inch from one end (Fig. 27-3). This is for the air to enter and will be the front of the gauge. Cut another piece of styrofoam and plug the end of the straw below the notch. Next, cut a small hole in the side of the straw near

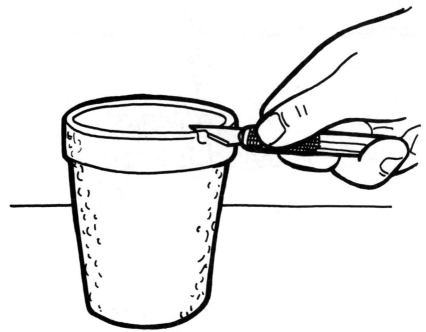

Fig. 27-1. *Cut out a small piece of styrofoam to make the ball.*

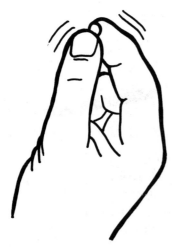

Fig. 27-2. *Roll the styro-foam between your fingers to make it round.*

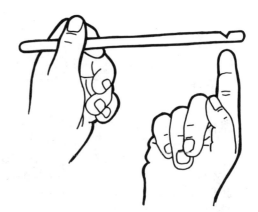

Fig. 27-3. *Cut a notch for the air to enter.*

the opening at the other end of the straw. This is to let air escape when you are measuring higher winds.

Place the straw on the center of the cardboard with the notch facing forward and press one of the pins through the straw and cardboard, just above the notch. Drop the ball into the other end of the straw and press the other pin through the straw and the cardboard, just below the small hole you cut for the high range. Fasten the straw to the cardboard with a couple of strips of transparent tape (Fig. 27-4).

To calibrate your wind gauge, hold it outside a car window on a calm day. Have the open notch at the bottom of the straw facing into the wind. Air entering here will lift the styrofoam ball to various heights in the straw depending on the speed of the air. Use the speedometer to mark the card. For higher wind speeds, hold your finger over the top of the straw. This will keep the ball from rising as high and forces the air to leave through the small hole you cut near the top.

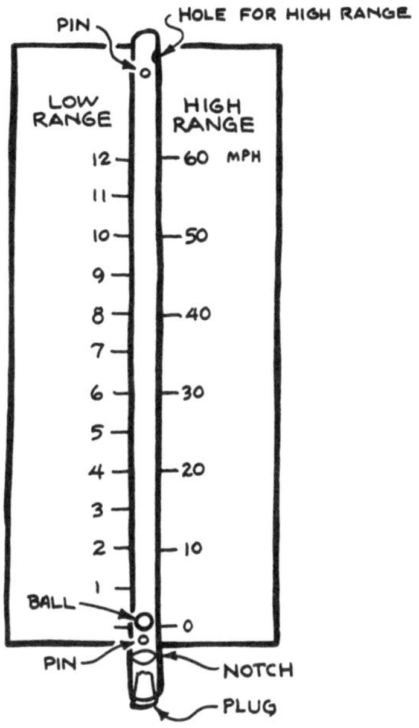

Fig. 27-4. Front view of a completed wind gauge.

28

Wind Currents and Mountains

Materials

electric fan
stack of books
different sizes
strip of tissue paper

Place the books in a stack to form a miniature mountain (Fig. 28-1). Set the fan a few feet from the books so that it blows a strong breeze over the stack (Fig. 28-2). Now, hold one end of the tissue paper so that it streams out over the books (Fig. 28-3).

Notice that on the side nearest the fan, the wind rises up, while on the side away from the fan, the wind suddenly descends. The side next to the fan is called the windward side and the side away from the fan is called the lee side. Weather reporting stations provide wind direction and speed for aircraft pilots so that they know which side of the mountains has the downdrafts and which side has the updrafts.

Fig. 28-1. *Stack a few books to form the shape of a mountain.*

Fig. 28-2. *Use a fan to create the wind.*

Fig. 28-3. *Tissue paper will show the wind currents.*

Mountain ranges can alter the temperature and direction of the prevailing winds. Near the coast, they can block ocean breezes from inland areas. Mountains in western Washington and Oregon block the rain-bearing winds from the Pacific Ocean. This keeps the eastern side of these states dry while the western part is wet (Fig. 28-4).

Fig. 28-4. *Mountains can block moisture-carrying winds.*

29

How to Make a Rain Gauge

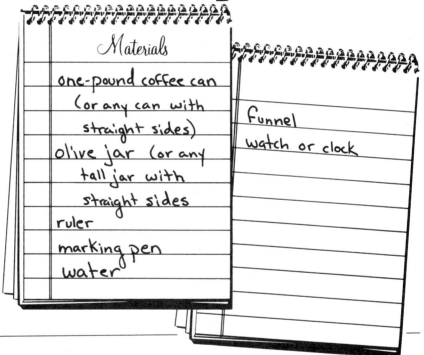

Materials

one-pound coffee can
(or any can with
straight sides)
olive jar (or any
tall jar with
straight sides
ruler
marking pen
water

funnel
watch or clock

Place the end of the ruler into the can and pour in water to a depth of 2 inches (Fig. 29-1). Place the funnel in the olive jar and pour the 2 inches of water from the can into the jar (Fig. 29-2). Mark the level of the water on the outside of the jar (Fig. 29-3). Pour out the water. Now use the ruler to divide the space below the mark you made into 20 equal spaces (Fig. 29-4). This will divide the space into tenths, with each mark representing one-tenth of an inch of rain.

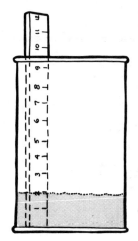

Fig. 29-1. Pour 2 inches of water into the can.

Fig. 29-2. Pour the water into the olive jar.

Fig. 29-3. Mark the level on the jar.

Now, just before a rain, place the coffee can in an open area away from trees and buildings (Fig. 29-5). Notice the time it starts to rain and when it stops. After the rain stops, use the funnel to pour the rainwater from the can into the jar (Fig. 29-6). Read the marks on the jar to determine the amount of rain that fell. The time you noted will give you the rate of the rainfall.

Fig. 29-4. *Divide the space into 20 equal spaces.*

Fig. 29-5. *Place the can in an open area.*

Fig. 29-6. *Pour the rainwater into the olive jar.*

30

How to Measure Snowfall as Precipitation

Materials

two-pound coffee can
(or any can with
straight sides and
about 12 inches tall)

olive jar gauge
(see Experiment 29)

ruler

snow

Fill the can with loose snow. Don't pack it in. Use the ruler and measure the depth of the snow (Fig. 30-1). Now take the can to a warm place and let the snow melt (Fig. 30-2). Pour the water from the snow into your rain gauge and see how many inches of water the snow made (Fig. 30-3). You should find that it takes about a foot of snow to equal one inch of rain.

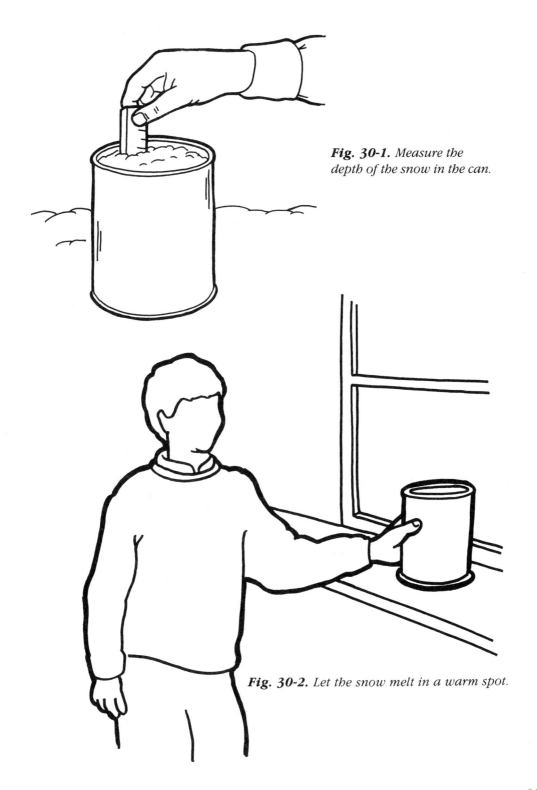

Fig. 30-1. Measure the depth of the snow in the can.

Fig. 30-2. Let the snow melt in a warm spot.

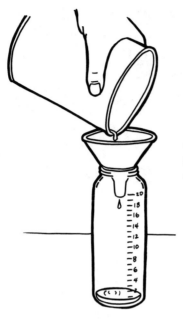

Fig. 30-3. Use your rain gauge to measure the amount of precipitation.

31

How to Make a Hair Hygrometer

Materials

piece of wood (2×4
about 12 inches long)
3 strands of human hair
(about 10 inches long)
cardboard pointer
(about 3 inches long)
pin or tack
glue

pencil
ruler

A hygrometer is an instrument meteorologists use to measure the humidity of the atmosphere.

Use the pin and mount the larger end of the pointer to the flat side of the wood (Fig. 31-1). Attach the pointer so that the small end is free to move up and down. Twist the hairs a little so that they are together (Fig. 31-2) and glue one end to the pointer about a fourth of an inch from the pin (Fig. 31-3).

Move the pointer so that it is level and glue the other end of the hair near the top of the piece of wood. The strands of hair should run straight up and down and should support the pointer. Use the

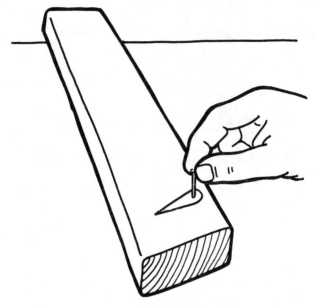

Fig. 31-1. *Mount the pointer to the piece of wood.*

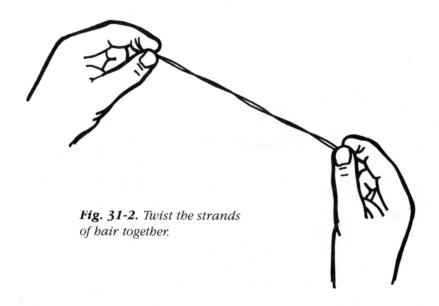

Fig. 31-2. *Twist the strands of hair together.*

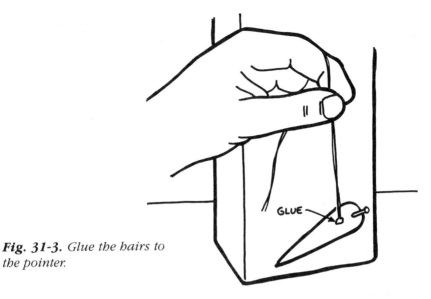

Fig. 31-3. *Glue the hairs to the pointer.*

ruler and mark a few lines of equal spaces for the pointer (Fig. 31-4).

Now, as the moisture in the air increases, the hairs will expand and the pointer will move down. As the air becomes dryer, the hairs contract and the pointer will move up. This will give you an approximate idea of the relative humidity.

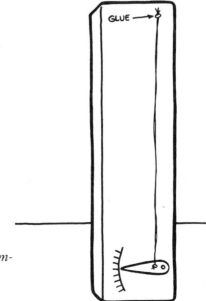

Fig. 31-4. *View of completed hair hygrometer.*

32

How to Make a Psychrometer

Materials

2 thermometers
cardboard (about
4 x 10 inches)
masking tape
small piece of cotton
cloth (muslin)
rubber band
string
water

A psychrometer is an instrument with wet and dry bulb thermometers for measuring moisture in the air. The wet bulb helps determine the relative humidity.

Use the tape to securely mount the two thermometers side by side on the cardboard. Mount them so that the bulb ends extend past the end of the cardboard and one bulb end extends just past the other. Make a small hole in the cardboard near the end with the tops of the thermometers. Tie one end of the string through this hole (Fig. 32-1). Now wrap the small piece of cloth around the bulb of the thermometer sticking farthest from the end of the cardboard.

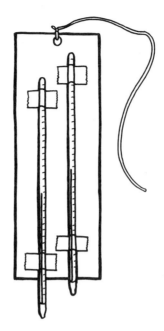

Fig. 32-1. Mount the thermometers on the card.

The cloth will hold the moisture for the wet bulb thermometer. Fasten the cloth in place with the rubber band (Fig. 32-2). This will be the wet bulb thermometer and the other will be the dry bulb thermometer.

Dip the cloth attached to the thermometer in water (Fig. 32-3) and then swing the thermometers in the air for about a minute (Fig. 32-4). Now quickly read the wet bulb thermometer and then the dry bulb thermometer. Now read horizontally across the top of the chart to find the number representing the wet bulb temperature (Table 32-1). Then read downward on the left side to the dry bulb temperature. The numbers found at that intersection will be the dew point in Fahrenheit degrees and the relative humidity in percents.

When you whirl the psychrometer through the air, water in the cloth evaporates and cools the wet bulb. The amount of cooling depends on the relative humidity. The lower the humidity, the faster the water will evaporate and the more the bulb will cool. High humidity causes less evaporation and slows the cooling process. This is why it can be uncomfortable on a summer day that is 85 degrees with 90 percent humidity in one area and quite pleasant in another area that is 85 degrees with only 20 percent humidity.

Fig 32-2. *Attach the cloth to the wet bulb thermometer.*

Fig. 32-3. *Wet the cloth in the water.*

Fig. 32-4. *Swing the thermometers in the air.*

Table 32-1. *If the wet bulb temperature is 51 and the dry bulb temperature is 68, the dew point will be 34°F and the relative humidity will be 28 percent.*

WET BULB TEMPERATURES

Each cell shows the dew point (top number) over the relative humidity (bottom number).

DRY BULB	42	43	44	45	46	47	48	49	50	51	52	53	54	55	56	57
66	-28 / 2	-7 / 5	+4 / 8	11 / 12	17 / 15	22 / 19	26 / 22	30 / 26	33 / 30	36 / 33	39 / 37	42 / 41	44 / 45	46 / 49	49 / 53	51 / 58
67		-15 / 3	-1 / 6	+8 / 10	15 / 13	20 / 16	24 / 20	28 / 23	32 / 27	35 / 31	38 / 34	41 / 38	43 / 42	46 / 46	48 / 50	50 / 54
68		-29 / 2	-7 / 5	+4 / 8	12 / 11	18 / 14	22 / 18	27 / 21	30 / 24	34 / 28	37 / 32	40 / 35	42 / 39	45 / 43	47 / 47	49 / 51
69			-15 / 3	-1 / 6	+8 / 9	15 / 12	20 / 16	25 / 19	29 / 22	32 / 26	35 / 29	38 / 33	41 / 36	44 / 40	46 / 44	48 / 47
70			-29 / 1	-7 / 4	+4 / 7	12 / 10	18 / 14	23 / 17	27 / 20	31 / 23	34 / 27	37 / 30	40 / 34	43 / 37	45 / 41	47 / 44
71				-15 / 3	0 / 6	+9 / 9	15 / 12	21 / 15	25 / 18	29 / 21	33 / 24	36 / 28	39 / 31	42 / 34	44 / 38	46 / 42
72				-28 / 1	-6 / 4	+5 / 7	12 / 10	18 / 13	23 / 16	28 / 19	31 / 22	35 / 25	38 / 29	40 / 32	43 / 35	46 / 39
73					-14 / 3	0 / 5	+9 / 8	16 / 11	21 / 14	26 / 17	30 / 20	33 / 23	36 / 26	39 / 30	42 / 33	45 / 36
74					-27 / 1	-6 / 4	+5 / 7	13 / 10	19 / 12	24 / 15	28 / 18	32 / 21	35 / 24	38 / 27	41 / 30	44 / 34
75						-13 / 3	+1 / 5	10 / 8	16 / 11	22 / 13	26 / 16	30 / 19	34 / 22	37 / 25	40 / 28	43 / 31
76						-25 / 1	-5 / 4	+6 / 7	14 / 9	20 / 12	24 / 15	29 / 17	32 / 20	36 / 23	39 / 26	42 / 29
77						-57	-12 / 3	+2 / 5	10 / 8	17 / 10	22 / 13	27 / 16	31 / 18	34 / 21	38 / 24	41 / 27
78							-27 / 1	-4 / 4	+7 / 6	14 / 9	20 / 11	25 / 14	29 / 17	33 / 19	36 / 22	39 / 25
79							-48	-11 / 3	+3 / 5	11 / 8	18 / 10	23 / 13	28 / 15	32 / 18	35 / 20	38 / 23
80								-21 / 2	-2 / 4	+8 / 6	15 / 9	21 / 11	26 / 14	30 / 16	34 / 19	37 / 21
81								-40 / 1	-9 / 3	+4 / 5	12 / 7	19 / 10	24 / 12	28 / 15	32 / 17	36 / 20
82									-18 / 2	-1 / 4	+9 / 6	16 / 8	22 / 10	27 / 13	31 / 16	34 / 18
83									-34 / 1	-7 / 3	+5 / 5	13 / 7	20 / 9	25 / 12	29 / 14	33 / 17
84										-15 / 2	+1 / 4	10 / 6	17 / 8	23 / 10	27 / 13	
85										-29 / 1	-5 / 3	+7 / 5	14 / 7	21 / 9	26 / 11	
86											-12 / 2	+2 / 4	11 / 6	18 / 8	24 / 10	
87											-24 / 1	-3 / 3	+8 / 5	16 / 7	22 / 9	

DRY BULB TEMPERATURES

Legend:

```
 34  →  DEW POINT
 38  →  RELATIVE HUMIDITY
```

33

How to Make a Barometer

Materials

tall, clear glass or jar
bowl
4 paper clips
water

A barometer is an instrument used to measure the pressure of the atmosphere. It is especially helpful in determining weather changes.

Slip the paper clips onto the rim of the glass. Space them equal distances around the rim, and press them down next to the glass (Fig. 33-1). Fill the glass about two-thirds full of water. Place the bowl upside down over the glass (Fig. 33-2). Turn the bowl and the glass of water rightside up. Some of the water will run into the bowl and the rest of the water will remain in the glass (Fig. 33-3). Mark

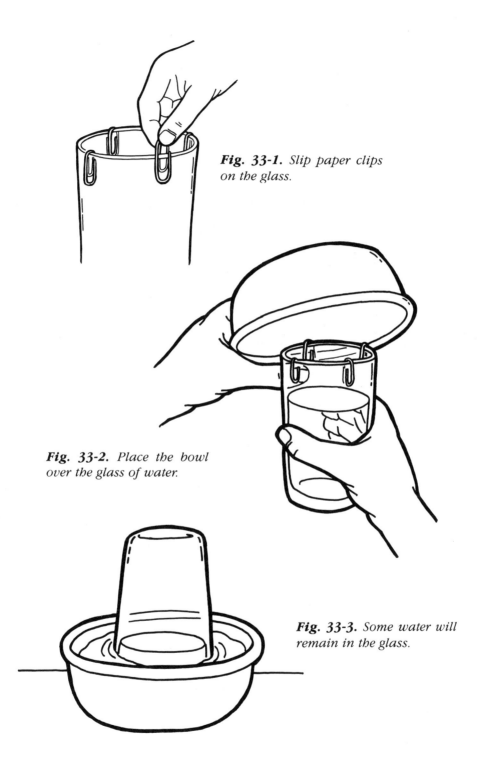

Fig. 33-1. Slip paper clips on the glass.

Fig. 33-2. Place the bowl over the glass of water.

Fig. 33-3. Some water will remain in the glass.

the level of the water in the glass and set the bowl outside (Fig. 33-4). As the weather changes, the atmospheric pressure changes and the water will rise and fall in the glass. If the water level drops, this might mean a low pressure area and a storm is approaching. If the water level rises, it could indicate a high pressure area and probably means fair weather.

Meteorologists refer to areas of different air pressures as highs or lows. A barometer is simply an instrument that measures these air pressures. A barometer that is commercially made will be much more accurate than your homemade one, but your barometer will demonstrate the principle of how they work.

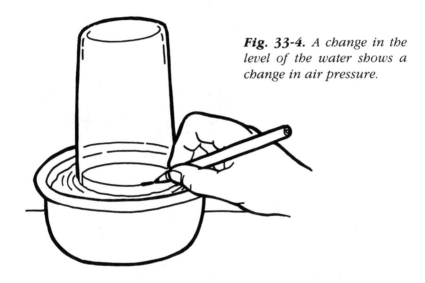

Fig. 33-4. A change in the level of the water shows a change in air pressure.

34

Measuring the Distance to a Storm

Materials

watch with
second hand
thunderstorm

Watch for a flash of lightning and count the number of seconds until you hear the thunder (Fig. 34-1). Now divide the number of seconds by five. This will give you the approximate number of miles to the storm.

Light from the flash travels to your eyes almost instantly, while the sound travels at about 1,100 feet per second (Fig. 34-2). If you counted 5 seconds, the distance to the lightning was about 5,500 feet, or a little more than one mile. If you don't have a watch, simply count "thousand one, thousand two, thousand three, thousand four," and so on. Each count will represent one second and five seconds will represent one mile.

Fig. 34-1. *Count the number of seconds until you hear thunder.*

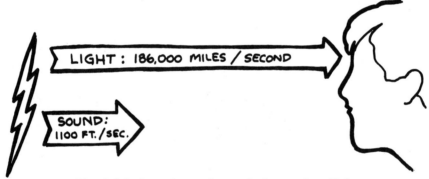

LIGHT : 186,000 MILES / SECOND

SOUND: 1100 FT./SEC.

Fig. 34-2. *Sound travels much slower than light.*

35

How to Read
a Weather Map

Materials

weather map
from newspaper

The lines on a weather map indicate areas of equal air pressures. They are called isobars (Fig. 35-1). The farther apart these lines are, the lighter the winds. When these lines are close together, the pressure is normally low and the winds strong. Maps usually have keys over to one side that display symbols that represent the various weather conditions. This will include showers, rain, thunderstorms, and snow flurries. There will also be symbols that represent cold fronts, warm fronts and stationary fronts.

An area of high pressure can be thought of as a mountain of air. It is heavier and rises above the surrounding air mass. Winds in a

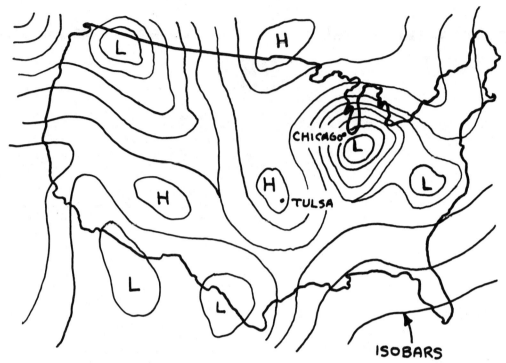

Fig. 35-1. *Isobars are lines showing areas of equal air pressure.*

high pressure area spiral outward and downward. This causes clouds to evaporate and usually brings fair weather. An area of low pressure can be thought of as a valley. It is lighter than the surrounding air mass and causes winds to spiral inward. This makes the air in the center of the low rise. This rising air cools and often condenses into fog, clouds, or rain. Lows usually bring wet, stormy weather (Fig. 35-2).

A cold front occurs when a mass of cold air pushes its way underneath a warmer mass of air (Fig. 35-3). This forces the warm air upward and, as the front moves, the cold air replaces the warm air. This allows a narrow line of clouds to form along the front and violent rainstorms can occur.

A warm front forms when a mass of warm air overtakes, and rides over, the top of a mass of cold air (Fig. 35-4). This causes clouds and sometimes violent thunderstorms to form in a wide area of the front.

By looking at the weather map shown, you can see that Tulsa probably has clear skies while Chicago should have rain and high winds.

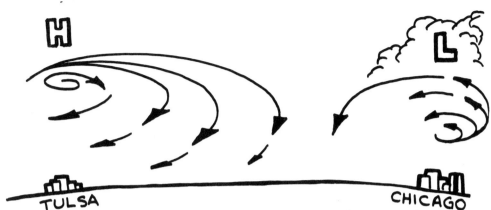

Fig. 35-2. *High pressure areas can be thought of as mountains.*

COLD FRONT

Fig. 35-3. *A cold front occurs when a mass of cold air pushes under a warmer mass of air.*

WARM FRONT

Fig. 35-4. *A warm front occurs when a mass of warm air slides over the top of a mass of cold air.*

36

How to Predict Changes in the Weather

Materials

barometer
magnetic compass

Carefully observe wind directions and barometric readings and notice any cloud formations (Fig. 36-1).

If the wind blows gently from the west or northwest, and the barometer reading is steady or rises, the weather should continue to be fair (Fig. 36-2).

If the wind is blowing from the south or southwest, and the barometer begins to fall, you might notice altocumulus clouds building near the north or northwest horizon. This often means that a storm is approaching (Fig. 36-3).

Fig. 36-1. *Observe wind directions and barometric readings.*

WIND FROM
WEST/N.W.

BAROMETER
RISING

Fig. 36-2. *A gentle west wind and a rising barometer usually means continued fair weather.*

Fig. 36-3. *A south wind and a falling barometer could mean an approaching storm.*

If the wind is blowing from a southeasterly direction, the barometer is dropping, and the sky is completely covered with dull-gray altostratus clouds, this can mean continued rain or snow (Fig. 36-4).

If it is a clear night and a light wind is blowing from the north or northwest, and the barometer is steadily rising, the temperature will probably begin to fall (Fig. 36-5).

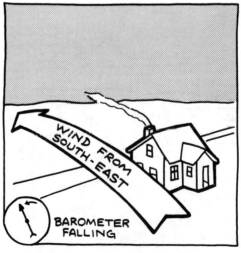

Fig. 36-4. *Continued rain or snow can be indicated by a dull, gray cloud cover, a falling barometer, and a southeasterly wind.*

Fig. 36-5. *A clear night, a gentle wind from the north, and a rising barometer can mean that the temperature will start to drop.*

37

Why Birds Roost Before a Storm

Materials

an observation

Air normally moves from a high pressure area into a low pressure area (Fig. 37-1). This means that winds usually blow out of a high into a low. Lows generally bring cloudy or stormy weather. Birds often begin to roost just before a storm because they have difficulty flying in the thin, light air that is usually present just before a storm (Fig. 37-2).

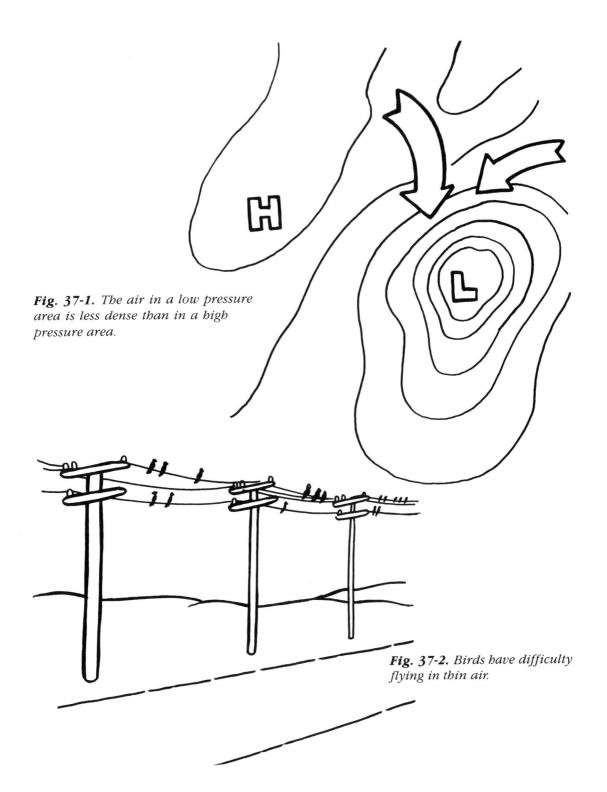

Fig. 37-1. *The air in a low pressure area is less dense than in a high pressure area.*

Fig. 37-2. *Birds have difficulty flying in thin air.*

38

Aching Corns and Bad Weather

Materials

an observation

When the air pressure begins to fall, tissues inside the body start to swell. This often causes pain at sensitive spots, such as in arthritic joints or corns. In this way, aching corns or other pains can sometimes forecast bad weather (Fig. 38-1).

Fig. 38-1. *Tissues inside our body begin to swell when the air pressure begins to fall.*

39

Other Forecasters of Bad Weather

Materials

an observation

When the pressure begins to fall before the arrival of bad weather, ants start to move to higher ground (Fig. 39-1) and sheep's wool starts to uncurl (Fig. 39-2). Pine cones open when rain is near (Fig. 39-3) and frogs croak more when the pressure drops (Fig. 39-4). The lower pressure outside the bodies of things causes the inside pressure to increase. This increase in pressure allows animals to sense the approach of storms and causes pine cones to open.

Weather forecasts depend on observations made at weather stations throughout the world. Meteorologists analyze the information and base their forecasts on the patterns that highs and lows

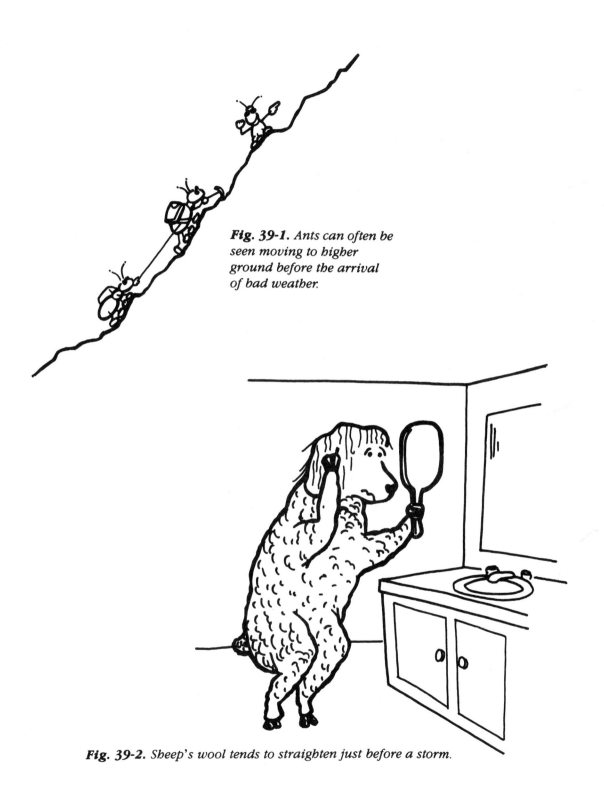

Fig. 39-1. Ants can often be seen moving to higher ground before the arrival of bad weather.

Fig. 39-2. Sheep's wool tends to straighten just before a storm.

Fig. 39-3. *Pinecones open to catch rain.*

Fig. 39-4. *Frogs usually croak more when the barometer falls.*

usually follow. They use sensitive instruments and computers to provide weather forecasts we see on television and read in the newspaper. The U.S. Weather Bureau continuously monitors the weather and makes numerous forecasts each day. It also sends out storm and flood warnings as well as severe weather warnings that include tornadoes and hurricanes.

PART II

SCIENCE FAIRS

A science fair project can be an exciting learning experience, but it does require some planning. Not enough to fret over but a little organization and planning is necessary if you want the project to be successful. One of the most important parts of the planning stage is deciding on the subject. Do some research and give the subject a lot of thought. If you choose a subject too quickly, you might discover later that the materials are too expensive or not even available, or that the project was just too complicated to complete. When this happens, it is too easy to abandon the project and it is usually too late to start another.

You may want to start by dividing your science fair project into four easy steps:

1. Choosing a subject.

2. Questions and hypothesis. A hypothesis is just what you think the results of the experiment will be—a well-thought-out guess.

3. Doing the experiment.

4. The results and your conclusions.

You might want to write a research paper (Fig. 1). The research paper will help you gather important information and narrow down your subject to a specific topic. You probably want to make a report on your experiment. This is to show what you wanted to

Fig. 1. A research paper will help you gather information.

prove or a question you wanted answered. You can use graphs and charts to help explain your project. The report should describe your experiment, the results of your experiment, and the conclusions you formed based on the results of the experiment.

When deciding on a project, pick a subject that you are really interested in, or one that you would like to learn more about. Choose a subject that you are enthused about, but not one that is too complicated. You might find problems locating the materials. A simple, well demonstrated experiment can be much more successful than a complicated one not performed well. Often, major scientific breakthroughs are discovered using simple equipment.

Materials for experiments can often be throwaway items found around the home, such as empty coffee cans, plastic or glass bottles, cardboard tubes from paper towels, or empty wooden spools from sewing thread (Fig. 2).

Fig. 2. *Throwaway items can often be used in experiments.*

You might want to build a model. Usually, these can be made from wood or cardboard. You have to be creative and use your imagination.

Once you have selected the subject of your project, choose a specific question to be answered or a point to prove. Don't generalize. Have a definite problem to solve. For example, if you wanted to demonstrate something about winds, you could build a model that would show how dense, cold air sinks and pushes up the lighter, warm air (Fig. 3).

If you were interested in something to do with cold, you could build a model to show why lakes don't freeze solid. This would show that water is one of the few things that expands when it freezes, allowing the ice to form at the surface (Fig. 4). Or you could build a hair hygrometer to show how much moisture is in the air (Fig. 5).

You probably will want to display your experiment on a table. It could be set up in front of cardboard or wooden panels (Fig. 6).

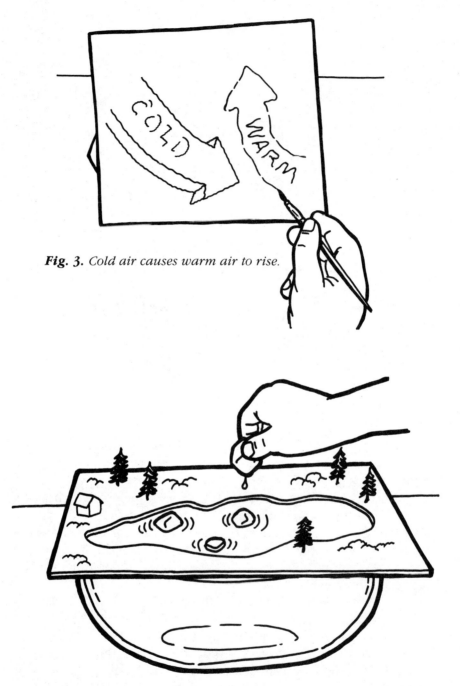

Fig. 3. *Cold air causes warm air to rise.*

Fig. 4. *Lakes would freeze solid if water didn't expand when it freezes.*

Fig. 5. *A hair hygrometer will show how much moisture is in the air.*

Fig. 6. *An attractive background can provide information about your project.*

The panels could be in three sections. The two end sections might be angled forward so that the panel stands by itself, like the back part of a theater stage. The panel sections can show the information from your report. The left section could show the purpose of your experiment. This could include why you chose the project or what you wanted to prove. The middle section of the panel could show how your experiment was constructed and why it was built the way it was. The right section of the panel could show the results of your experiment and the conclusions you've made. It could also include any possible uses, or applications for, this information.

If you use your imagination, you can expand and develop any simple experiment into a very interesting and educational project. Most any experiment will probably have been done before, but yours might be just a little different. Try to use a different point of view, or change a known experiment so that you prove something completely different. The important part of a science fair project is to have fun while you discover something new.

Glossary

air mass A huge mass of cold or warm air that moves around the world. It can can be moist or dry.

altocumulus cloud A formation of white or gray clouds in many shapes, most commonly rounded, found at intermediate heights.

altostratus cloud A formation of gray to bluish clouds found at intermediate heights in continuous dense layers or thick patches.

atmosphere The mass of air, clouds, gases, and vapor, surrounding the earth.

atmospheric pressure The pressure caused by gravity of the blanket of air around the earth.

barometer An instrument for measuring atmospheric pressure. It is helpful in determining weather changes.

calibrate To fix, check, or correct the graduations of a measuring instrument, such as a thermometer.

celsius degrees (°C) used for measuring temperature, also called centigrade.

centigrade *See also* celsius.

circumference The line marking the boundary of a circle or a rounded surface.

cirrus cloud A formation of clouds in detached, wispy filaments, or feathery tufts, at heights above 20,000 feet. Often signs of bad weather to come.

cloud   A visible mass of condensed water vapor suspended in the atmosphere and consisting of minute droplets or ice crystals.

cold fronts   Boundaries between two different air masses caused when cold air pushes warm air away; usually means colder weather.

compressed air   Air reduced in volume by pressure and held in a container.

concentrated   collected or focused where the strength, or density, is increased.

condensation   The act of condensing, as the reduction of a gas to a liquid.

condense   To change a substance to a denser form, as from a gas to a liquid.

contract   Shrink in size.

convection currents   Currents that flow when lighter warm air rises and heavier cool air flows in to take its place.

Coriolis force   The force created by the bending of the winds caused by the earth spinning on its axis.

cumulonimbus cloud   A dense cloud towering to great heights, with the upper portion usually flattened. Often produces lightning and heavy showers.

cumulus cloud   A thick cloud, usually isolated, with a dark, nearly horizontal base. The upper parts resemble domes or towers.

dense   Having the parts crowded or packed tightly together.

dew point   The temperature at which condensation begins to form because the air cannot hold any more water vapor.

downdraft   A downward flow of air caused by convection currents or the down-wind side of mountains.

equatorial calm   When warm air over the equator moves upward and is not felt as wind.

equatorial low   A low pressure area caused by the warm air rising over the equator.

evaporation   When liquid water is heated and turns into water vapor.

exosphere   The layer that includes all air beyond 120 miles above the earth.

expand   To become greater, or larger, in size.

Fahrenheit   Degrees (°F) used for measuring temperature.

fog   A large mass of water vapor condensed into fine particles near the earth's surface.

freezing point   The temperature at which a liquid freezes or becomes a solid. The freezing point of water is 32° F.

frost   Frozen dew or vapor.

highs   Areas of high pressure that normally bring dry weather.

humidity   The amount of moisture in the form of water vapor contained in the air.

hygrometer   An instrument used to measure humidity.

hypothesis   A guess used by scientists to explain how or why something happens.

ionosphere   The layer of air from 60 to 120 miles up.

isobars   Lines drawn on a weather map that join places of equal air pressure.

lows   Areas of low pressure that often bring wet weather.

molecules   The smallest particle of an element or compound that can exist in the free state, and still retain the traits of the element or compound.

nimbus cloud   A rain-producing cloud.

prevailing winds   The strongest, most frequent winds in an area.

psychrometer   An instrument with wet and dry bulb thermometers for measuring moisture in the air. The dry bulb indicates the temperature of the air. The wet bulb helps determine the relative humidity.

radiation   The process in which energy in the form of rays of light, heat, etc., is sent out through space.

relative humidity   The amount of moisture in the air compared with the maximum amount of moisture that the air could hold at the same temperature, expressed as a percentage.

saturated   Having absorbed all that can be taken out.

stratosphere   The layer of air from 10 miles to 60 miles up.

stratus cloud   A cloud extending in a long, low, gray layer with an almost uniform base. Often brings drizzle and can cover high ground and cause hill fog.

trade winds   Winds that blow steadily toward the equator from the northeast in the tropics north of the equator and from the southeast in the tropics south of the equator.

troposphere   The layer of air from the earth to about 10 miles up.

updraft   An upward flow of air caused by convection currents or the up-wind side of mountains.

volume   A space occupied by matter.

warm fronts   Boundaries between two different air masses caused when warm air pushes cold air away; usually means warmer weather.

Index